BRITAIN IN OLD PHOTOGRAPHS

SUFFOLK AT WORK

ROBERT MALSTER

ALAN SUTTON PUBLISHING LIMITED

Alan Sutton Publishing Limited
Phoenix Mill · Far Thrupp · Stroud
Gloucestershire · GL5 2BU

Suffolk County Council

First published 1995

Cover photograph: *(front)* Ernie Nunn standing in front of a steam ploughing engine (see p. 24); *(back)* two blacksmiths tyring a wheel.

British Library Cataloguing in Publication Data.
A catalogue record for this book is available from the British Library.

ISBN 0-7509-0845-9

Typeset in 9/10 Sabon.
Typesetting and origination by
Alan Sutton Publishing Limited.
Printed in Great Britain by
Ebenezer Baylis, Worcester.

To the memory of Pat Woodgate

Contents

Shooting the nets on the Lowestoft motor drifter *Harold Cartwright* during the 1953 Home Fishing. The mate has just cast the first net overboard with a muttered 'Uvver she goo in the Name o' the Lord'. Within ten years the Home Fishing was a matter of history.

Introduction

Some people have said that life in Suffolk is unchanging, but a careful inspection of old photographs such as those in this book show that this is far from true. Life on the farm and in the countryside has undergone a major revolution in this century, while at sea the decline and end of the herring fishery has led to the disappearance of a whole way of life in certain of the coastal communities.

The county is fortunate that almost fifty years ago Mr R.G. Pratt began gathering historic photographs of local scenes, farming activities, trades and industries, and events, as well as taking his own photographs. The Suffolk Local History Council (SLHC) was set up in 1953, and it in turn formed the Suffolk Photographic Survey (SPS). This collection was developed by the hard work of Bob Pratt, who devoted both time and effort to it.

Postcard collections belonging to his friends and fellow members of the SLHC were copied, prints were made from their negatives, and where they were available original negatives and prints of considerable age were added to the ever-growing archive. Indexing the photographs was a vital but difficult and time-consuming task.

When Bob and Jean Pratt moved to the West Country some twenty-five years ago the SPS, by then numbering some 8,000 photographs, was moved to the Abbot's Hall Museum of Rural Life at Stowmarket, now the Museum of East Anglian Life. During its stay there Mrs Ena Carter continued the task of indexing and researching the collection, which continued to grow.

Today the collection comprises more than 18,000 items and is housed in the Suffolk Record Office at Ipswich. It has become the joint responsibility of the Record Office and the SLHC. The great majority of the illustrations in this book have come from the SPS, with the sanction of the Record Office and the SLHC.

It had been intended that this book should cover all aspects of Suffolk at work, but because of the wealth of material available in the SPS and the great breadth of the subject I have restricted myself to farming and fishing, making it possible to look at these aspects in more detail than would otherwise have been possible. It is hoped that a further book dealing with crafts and industries, including basketmaking, rush weaving, brickmaking, malting, tanning, engineering and shipbuilding, will follow in due course.

My thanks go to David Jones and the staff of Suffolk Record Office for their invaluable help, to the many people who made photographs new and old available to the SPS, and perhaps most of all to Bob Pratt for having had the vision to set it up almost half a century ago.

For their help with my research into the background of the pictures and for their encouragement I have innumerable people to thank, but particularly Jack Carter, president of the SLHC, David Cleveland, archivist of the East Anglian Film Archive, Hector Moore and Mrs Moore, of Brandeston, and Mrs Valerie Norrington, secretary of the SLHC.

My thanks are also due to Mrs Pat Woodgate, who in the course of her work at the Record Office built up a deep and valuable knowledge of the photographic collection. With her I first discussed the idea of a book on the county's trades and industries, but unhappily she died in a road accident before that idea bore fruit. It is to her memory that I dedicate this book.

Robert Malster
Holbrook

A ploughing match at Mendlesham Lodge, 1929. Just look at the enjoyment on those faces! (SPS 6645)

Section One

FARMING LIFE

One of the dirtiest jobs on the farm was cleaning out a pond, like this deep one on the Knoll Meadow at Bushes Farm, Haughley, here being 'fied out' in 1930. Many ponds are now filled in, but they were formerly a vital part of the farm, providing not only a place for cattle and horses to drink but also a source of water for domestic purposes. (SPS 7082)

Over the past 100 years the nature of Suffolk agriculture has changed in a profound way. Before 1914 farming was labour-intensive, with as many as 33,000 workers employed on the land in about 1840 out of a 'labouring' population of under 40,000. The main source of power on the farm was the horse, a draught animal on which a whole culture depended.

Major Edward Moor described in 1823 how whole families found employment in 'droppen', that is, the operation of dropping grains of wheat, peas or beans into the holes made by dibbles held in each hand by the dibbler, the man of the family. 'Droppers are always women and children; and as the dibbler generally takes the job by the acre, the earnings of a family at this work are considerable,' the old East India Company Army officer recorded. 'It is surprising with what quickness and accuracy dropping is executed by a good dropper.'

Even at that time sowing by such means was being threatened by the spread of the seed drill, developed at Peasenhall by James Smyth, one of those 'ingenious mechanics' who were collaborating with innovative farmers to introduce machinery to the farm. The drills were drawn by horses, as were the ploughs and other implements made by Ransomes at Ipswich and by other firms scattered throughout the county.

By the end of the century, however, steam engines made by Ransomes, by Richard Garretts at Leiston and by Burrells at Thetford, among others, were taking over some of the tasks traditionally done by the horse. It was the beginning of a revolution which was in the twentieth century to sweep away an entire culture and to have a marked effect on the countryside itself.

Men trapping linnets to sell as songbirds, *c.* 1885. A linnet in a cage was popular in many a Victorian cottage, though the keeping of songbirds was later outlawed by legislation. The bird in the cage is a decoy bird used to attract wild birds to the traps, which were sprung by pulling on the strings held by the man on the left. (SPS 6839)

Chaff-cutting for fodder at Bildeston, using a machine made by Innis & Co. of Hitchin and owned, according to the plate on the machine, by 'A. Harvey, Bilderstone'. This appears to be Augustus Harvey, who at the beginning of the century was farming at Wattisham Hall, a mile and a half north-east of Bildeston. (SPS 8747)

Hedging was a winter job, being done here by Floyd Peecock at Wood Farm, Sibton, *c.* 1935. Keeping the hedges down to a manageable size was vital, and the operation also yielded material that could be used to lay bush drains; the brushwood laid in a trench and covered over with soil provided a channel for water to drain away. (East Anglian Film Archive)

Drainage was particularly important on the clay lands of High Suffolk, but even on the lighter soils the laying of drains was a vital part of farm improvement. By 1850 it was being said that throughout the entire heavy land of Suffolk there were very few arable fields in which drains were not to be found. The photographs on this and the next two pages are from quarter-plate glass negatives taken about 1900 by George Watkins, who farmed Hall and Abbey farms at Culpho, 4 miles west of Woodbridge; one assumes the operation was being carried out on his own land, and the workers were his employees. (SPS 452)

Draining: using the bottom spade to cut the narrow bottom of the trench. (SPS 453)

Sam Church using the scoop to level the bottom of the trench. (SPS 454)

Placing earthenware pipes made in a local brickworks into the trench bottom. Such pipes became more popular after the removal of the tax on bricks and pipes in 1850. (SPS 451)

This photograph is taken facing in the opposite direction to the previous one. The worker is using a hooked tool to pull the pipes up tight towards each other. (SPS 455)

Mole draining with a modern crawler tractor at Old Newton. The driver is about to drop the 'mole' by pulling on the cord at the back of his tractor. Mole draining was practised in the nineteenth century using a windlass operated either by manpower or by horse to haul the mole across a field. (SPS 7900/7)

When farming was mixed, both cattle and arable, there was a ready supply of farmyard manure to be spread on the fields. The 'muck' was carted by tumbril, deposited in heaps and then spread around using a muck fork, as seen in this still from one of Mary Field's films made in the mid-1930s. (East Anglian Film Archive)

In High Suffolk it was said that five heaps went to the load, twenty loads to the acre. Spreading the muck could be a back-breaking task, as were so many jobs on the farm. (East Anglian Film Archive)

Section Two

TO PLOUGH AND SOW

Ploughing at Dial Farm, Earl Soham, c. 1905. The farmer, George Turner, is at the plough and Charles Booty is leading the near horse, a colt being broken in. The plough is an AY made by James Bendall at Woodbridge in 1869. Great pride was taken in the quality of ploughing, an operation that was vital to the production of the following year's crops. (SPS 6369)

A ploughing demonstration at Nacton by Ransomes in the 1860s, with an RNF plough of the type that won the top prizes at the Royal Agricultural Society's Newcastle show in 1864; this type became known as the Newcastle plough. Robert Ransome, who set up business in Ipswich in 1789, patented the chilling process for ploughshares in 1803 and specialized in the production of ploughs. In the mid-nineteenth century the firm benefited greatly from the expertise of James Barker, champion ploughman of England, who earned himself more than £2,000 in prize money while demonstrating Ransomes' ploughs. (SPS 1695)

A wooden Suffolk swing-plough being conveyed along a road on its sled or, as pronounced in Suffolk, a 'slod'. This is said to have been the last surviving use in England of a wheelless vehicle once much more widely used in the countryside. One horse hauls the plough, while the other is led by the ploughman. (SPS 2352)

Ploughing at Hintlesham with a Cornish & Lloyd GCD plough, made at Risbygate Foundry, Bury St Edmunds. Although this plough has a single handle, a piece of wood inserted in a ring provides a rather makeshift second handle. The firm had been established in the nineteenth century by George Cornish as engineers, ironfounders, millwrights, boilermakers and agricultural implement manufacturers. (SPS 2335)

William Wilson's steam ploughing engines at Baylham, with foreman Dick Nightingale standing on the footplate of the first engine and Ernie Nunn in shirtsleeves standing in front of the second engine. William Wilson farmed at Baylham Hall throughout the first quarter of this century as well as at Darmsden and Barking. (SPS 796)

On previous pages: Steam cultivating at Battisford with tackle belonging to William Wilson, of Darmsden Hall, in the 1930s. A system of ploughing and cultivating by using a pair of engines was developed by John Fowler, with the assistance of William Worby, Ransomes' works manager. Although the first ploughing engines were built for him by Ransomes, Fowler eventually set up his own works in Leeds which produced large numbers of these impressive engines. (SPS 1544)

These photographs of Fowler Gyrotillers were taken in 1936 by Bob Pratt, who set up the Suffolk Photographic Survey. The brainchild of Norman Storey, a plantation manager in Puerto Rico, the Gyrotiller was designed to give excellent aeration of the soil without bringing the subsoil to the surface. The machine pictured above is on the road at Claydon, towing a living van which provided a home from home for its crew (SPS 2019), while the one below is at work at Capel St Mary (SPS 2230). These machines were operated by William and John Lockett Ltd, of Crowe Street, Stowmarket, who described themselves as gyrotilling contractors.

Various forms of harrow were employed to break up the soil and provide a fine tilth, and in some cases to root out weeds. In Suffolk early harrows were made of timber, with wooden or later with iron tines, but these were superseded by lighter implements made wholly of iron or steel. (East Anglian Film Archive)

A team of oxen at work at Theberton, *c.* 1885. Although it has been said that oxen were unsuitable for harrowing because of their uneven motion, they were certainly used on the lighter Suffolk lands. Because of their cloven hooves oxen had to have two shoes to each hoof, the edge of each shoe being turned up on the inside to avoid the shoe causing damage to the hoof. (SPS 2991)

The mid-nineteenth century saw the introduction of new implements such as Arthur Biddell's extirpating harrow, made in Ipswich by Ransomes, and his scarifier, 'used for the purpose of cultivating land . . . and bringing it into a proper state of tilth, much more effectually, and at less expense . . .'. This scarifier, closer in nature to the harrow than Biddell's wheeled implements, is in use at Coddenham in the late nineteenth century. (SPS 1381)

A wooden harrow in use at Chattisham. In spite of the activities of the agricultural implement makers some such primitive implements continued to be used well into the twentieth century. (SPS 2330)

Harrowing at Wherstead, 1955. The land here is light, but on heavier land three horses might be needed to draw a heavy harrow. (SPS 2016)

RANSOMES
"SMALL HOLDINGS"
CULTIVATOR
RANSOMES

Before the introduction of the seed drill crops were either dibbled or sown broadcast. In this film still from Mary Field's *This Was England*, made in 1935, William Aldred is broadcasting corn on a farm at Sibton. 'I've been a farming hand for forty years and I can sow seeds against anyone and I can sow ten acres of land with ten pints of seed,' he says in the film, which is a very early piece of documentary sound recording. (East Anglian Film Archive)

Opposite: An advertisement issued in about 1905 by Ransomes, Sims & Jefferies of Ipswich for one of their smaller cultivators. Best known for their part in plough development, this firm produced a wide range of implements for use in this country and for export all over the world. (Miss P. Waters)

Although the principle of the seed drill had been known at least since the beginning of the eighteenth century, it was the development carried out by the Smyths at Peasenhall and Sweffling at the beginning of the nineteenth century that made the drill a really practical and useful implement. The drill being used here at Culpho is drawn by four horses, a larger than usual number. (SPS 2357)

JAMES SMYTH & SONS LTD.,

WILL EXHIBIT AN ASSORTMENT OF THEIR

NONPAREIL" AND "SEMI-NONPAREIL" CORN DRILLS,

ALSO

MANURE AND SEED DRILLS.

FOR WHICH INSPECTION IS SOLICITED.

James Smyth & Sons' advertisement for one of their seed drills which appeared in local newspapers in 1904, when the Suffolk Show was at Bury St Edmunds. Based at Peasenhall in Suffolk, this firm had another works at Witham in Essex and showrooms in Paris at the beginning of this century, when it was sending its drills all over the world. The company closed down in 1967, supposedly because Smyth drills were everlasting and so many farmers were still using grandfather's old drill that sales dropped off. The real reason was, perhaps, more complex.

Drilling at Mr Thomas Williams' Mulletts Farm, Buxhall, *c.* 1900. Behind the drill is Robert Steed, driving is the farmer's son, E.W. Williams, and the boy is George Sparks; the nearside horse is Prince and the offside horse Bowler. (SPS 1867)

The seeds were delivered to the top of the seed chutes by small metal cups on a rotating axle driven by gears from a set of teeth on one of the wheels. Here the operator is tipping seed from a sack into a bushel 'hod' or measure, from which he can tip it into the seed box of the drill. (East Anglian Film Archive)

A drill in use at Leiston, 1935. The man following the drill with a 'spud' clears any coulter that becomes clogged. The coulter is the blade which makes the furrows into which the seed is dropped. In heavy land the sticky clay will build up on the coulter, affecting its performance and even blocking the seed aperture. It is unusual to have both a driver and a man walking beside the drill to steer it; normally the man steering the drill also drove. (East Anglian Film Archive)

Rolling a field of corn at Lower Abbey Farm, Leiston, 1935. Some farmworkers declared that this work, done in the spring as the weather became warmer, was one of the most pleasant jobs on the farm. (East Anglian Film Archive)

Section Three

TO REAP AND MOW

Harvest workers in the Hollesley area taking their 'bever' under the shade of a hedge, c. 1889. Haysel and then harvest were the culmination of the farming year, a time when the maximum possible number of workers was needed to bring in the harvest while the weather remained suitable. A gang of men such as this would sometimes 'take' the harvest at a price negotiated with the farmer, who would often agree to provide a 'horkey' or harvest feast at the end of harvest. (SPS 591)

Loading a wagon with hay at Henry Murrell's Windwhistle Farm, Earl Soham, in the 1920s. The man wearing a cloth cap on top of the load is Charles Smith. (SPS 2952)

Unloading the hay at Windwhistle Farm, Earl Soham. (SPS 6034A)

Mowing hay at Rattlesden using a mechanical mower, *c.* 1910. Such mowers were introduced in the 1850s, before which time mowing was carried out by hand using scythes. Machines were also developed for turning the hay as it lay drying in the meadow. (SPS 1864)

Stacking hay. In the foreground can be seen a stack base made of old railway materials; a base not only raised the hay off the ground to keep out the damp but also made it less easy for mice to reach the stack. (SPS 7856)

Men taking their 'bever' in the harvest field. The bever was the afternoon snack of the worker, more often referred to these days as 'fourses', from the time of day. The word comes from the Old French *beivre*. The horses on the left have greenstuff hung around their necks to discourage the flies; elder was considered particularly efficacious. (SPS 6847)

Mr Henry Reynolds' workers at White House Farm and Moat House Farm, Burgh, *c.* 1890. Left to right: James Blake, Jed Ablitt, David Crane, Sam Markham, Isaac Crane, Frank Pooley, John Blake, Alfred Ablitt, Arthur Ablitt, Ephraim Knoller (foreman). In front are others whose names have not been so carefully recorded. Note the cradles on the scythes, used when mowing wheat. (SPS 7302)

A team of reapers at Rattlesden, *c.* 1895. The photograph is most obviously posed, with the reapers supposedly whetting their scythes, but it does show how for every man with a scythe there was a second man gathering and tying sheaves, or shooves as they were called in Suffolk. (SPS 1863)

Harvesters at Spring Farm, Gislingham, farmed at the end of last century by Walter Coe. These men are mowing barley, and have bails on their scythes designed, like the cradles, to keep the corn erect and to lay it to one side so that it could easily be gathered into sheaves. (SPS 1545)

A harvest gang belonging to Edward Snell at Darmsden Hall, near Needham Market, soon after the turn of the century. Two have wooden rakes, used for raking up the straw, and the rest hold pitchforks; they are probably harvesting seed clover. (SPS 2546)

Harvesting at Tuddenham St Martin, August 1900. The workers are using a 'foot engine' or 'rack reaper', a mowing machine which gathered corn on a rack raised by the pressure of the foot on a pedal. When sufficient corn had been collected for a sheaf the rack was lowered and the corn pushed off using a special rake. Aubrey Mortimer is operating the machine, and a second man named Edwards wields the rake to push corn off the rack. (SPS 2263)

Taken at the same time, this photograph shows one man gathering up the corn while others in the background repair the broken-down reaper. (SPS 1713)

Harvesting with a sail reaper on Percy Warren's farm at Lawshall, 1902 or 1903. This implement was a development of the foot engine with 'sails' which automatically ejected the cut corn in intermittent swathes convenient for binding into sheaves. By the turn of the century about 80 per cent of the harvest was being cut by machine. The comparative thinness of the crop is noticeable in these photographs; 'you could see a blooda mouse runnin' about in that,' says a Suffolk man of the corn in these pictures. 'They'd get six coomb an acre then; today if you can't get three ton an acre you'd go out o' business.' (SPS 2351)

A group of harvesters at Tuddenham St Martin in 1900, with the rack reaper seen on p. 44. The man on the left holds the foot engine rake. One of the party is wearing an army slouch hat of the kind issued to the Imperial Yeomanry during the Boer War; the Suffolk Yeomanry (Loyal Suffolk Hussars) sent a detachment. (SPS 2233)

A self-binder in use at Hawkins' Farm, Mendlesham, 1926. As its name implies, the self-binder not only cut the corn but tied it into bundles using 'binder twine', a variety of coarse string. Note the 'coat' to protect the horse from insects. (SPS 6646)

Getting in the harvest at Waldringfield, as portrayed in a lantern slide made by the Revd T.N. Waller. The carter is thought to be George Brown. The windmill was operated in 1879 by William Buttrum, a member of a family which also ran mills at Woodbridge, Burgh, Hollesley and Swilland at that time; it was out of use by the turn of the century. (SPS 1707)

Harvesting beans at Letheringham, *c.* 1909. Back row, left to right: Nat Mattin, Jesse Titshall, Herbert Capon (the farmer), David Barnes, Charlie Peck, George Peck. Front row: -?-, Jerry Hammond, 'Young Capon', presumably the farmer's son. (SPS 5334)

Harvesting a catch crop of mustard using a Mogul tractor and a 5 foot binder, normally horse drawn, at Trucketts Farm, Boxted, early November 1916. Driving the tractor is Miss Balls, on the binder is Miss Harrison, and standing by is Ted Mason. (SPS 1986)

Harvesting with a self-binder at Holbrook in 1928, on land that was later to form the site for the Royal Hospital School. On the Fordson tractor is Warrenton Page, always known as 'Warry', and on the binder Walter Scott. (Mrs F. Wormald, Mrs M. Leeson)

A woman using a rake in the stackyard. Harvest was a time when there was a great demand for labour, and the womenfolk as well as the men found employment in the harvest field. (SPS 6379)

Women pulling flax at Whitings Farm, Mendlesham, *c.* 1916. In earlier times a good deal of both flax and hemp was grown in Suffolk, until the East Anglian linen industry declined in the face of competition from cotton. (SPS 6642)

Women pulling flax at Felsham during the First World War, when the growing of flax for the making of textiles was encouraged as a way of cutting the country's dependence on imports. (SPS 1968)

Wheat stacks at Stowupland Hall containing 100 to 120 coomb per stack, seen here in the mid-1930s. Ernie Brame used to make these stacks every year, and they were thatched by Alfred 'Happy' Robinson. (SPS 2239)

Stooking wheat at Grundisburgh, 1961. The stooks, or 'shocks' as they were usually called in Suffolk, stood in the field until the time came to cart them to the stackyard. 'Wheat is rarely fit for stacking in less than a week after it is cut, and in dull seasons it may require to be left a fortnight before it is safe to stack it,' according to an old farming handbook. A farmworker of the old school adds, 'They used to say you cut oats and you leave 'em in the field until they'd heard the church bells chime three times, that was three Sundays, then you could cart them.' (SPS 6080)

Building a stack at Boundary Farm, Needham Market, *c.* 1900. Construction of a stack was a highly skilled operation if both weather and vermin were to be kept out of the corn and it was to be maintained in good condition until the time came for threshing. (SPS 4668)

Building stacks, possibly at Culpho Hall, before the advent of mechanical aids such as elevators. In this case the stacks are not corn but peas, which are being pitched on to the top of the stack using pitchforks. (SPS 448)

Building a stack at Goodchild's Farm, Little Wenham, using a horse-operated elevator, photographed by Bob Pratt, who inaugurated the Suffolk Photographic Survey. (SPS 2956)

Some horse-operated elevators were converted to other sources of power. This one is being worked by an oil engine, typical of those which were to be found on many farms from the 1920s onwards. (SPS 6380)

A party of thatchers from Otley take a rest from their work at Cordle's farm at Chelmondiston, August 1962. They are, left to right, Russell Podd, Jim Stammers and Rowley Last, and the horseman is Ted Martin; he has probably just brought them a 'butt' of water for wetting the straw. Russell Podd also worked as a hurdlemaker (see p. 103). (SPS 2981)

Arthur Stone thatching a stack at Onehouse Hall Farm, *c.* 1949. His son, out of the picture, is preparing the straw. They took it in turns to thatch a stack, taking about a day to do one. (SPS 7184)

Section Four

A'TROSHEN

Threshing with flails at Great Oakley, a village in the Tendring Hundred, c. 1895. Although in Essex, the Tendring Hundred (that part of the north-east of the county just across the Stour from the Shotley Peninsula) has always had an affinity with Suffolk; as well as having their own Tendring Hundred Show its farmers regularly attend the Suffolk Show rather than the Essex. (SPS 2242)

Frank Pettitt threshing beans with a flail at Weybread, 1900. The flail, or the 'stick 'n' a half' as it was often called in Suffolk, continued to be used for some jobs well into the present century. (SPS 6768)

Taken in the Stowmarket area in the 1870s, this photograph shows a seed huller operated by a steam engine. Several men are holding the large baskets used to transfer the dressed grain; in earlier days they would have been employed in winnowing the seed. (SPS 2229)

A chain-driven Burrell engine of about 1869 belonging to James Ballam, of Mutton Hall, Wetherden, operating a thresher made by Marshall of Gainsborough in King's Field at Elmswell. (SPS 790)

A Garrett portable engine powering a Burrell threshing machine at Hill Farm, Iken, *c.* 1890. Note the water cart supplying water to the engine. The second Richard Garrett of Leiston married the daughter of John Balls, the inventor of the threshing drum (earlier threshers had been designed on a different principle), and the building of machines to Balls' design helped the Garrett firm in its nineteenth-century expansion. (SPS 127)

A portable engine operating thresher and elevator at White Hart Field, Otley, in the early years of the twentieth century. Left to right: Frank Fosdike, Ernest Borley (the owner of the threshing machine), William Fosdike, Tom Todd, Jim Garrod (farm bailiff for William Davey at Lane Farm, Swilland), Charles Fosdike, Thomas Davey, Philip Garrod, Charles Brown, Jerry Kemp. (SPS 11064)

A Ransomes, Sims & Jefferies portable engine working a thresher at Wenhaston, *c.* 1900. The engineman, Mr Burrows, has his hand on the regulator. (SPS 1556)

These three stills from Mary Field's *Farming in Winter* show the activity of threshing better than the old still photographs, mainly posed. A man on top of the machine feeds the drum; another brings large lumps of coal to the engine; and a third tends the sack into which the chaff is shot. Threshing needed quite a large labour force, whereas today a combine harvester operated by a single man both cuts and threshes the corn in a single operation. (East Anglian Film Archive).

When moving from one farm to another the engine hauled the threshing drum, the elevator and sometimes a living van as well. Here a Clayton and Shuttleworth engine with threshing train belonging to Philip Gage, of Chelsworth, is seen entering Semer Lodge, with Mr Grainger driving. (SPS 1835)

Workers gathered in front of a Burrell traction engine belonging to Alfred Dawson, of Rushmere St Andrew, at Butley, *c.* 1930. The firm of Alfred Dawson & Co. (Rushmere) Ltd, contractors for steam ploughing, cultivating, road rolling, haulage and threshing, and general engineers, had been founded in 1898 by the local miller who worked the windmill on the Playford Road. (SPS 3)

A steam traction engine engaged in threshing at Smeetham Hall, Sudbury, 1911. A water cart used to bring water for the engine's boiler is to be seen in the foreground. (SPS 1785)

Threshing at Brook Farm, Stutton, in the 1930s. This was hard, dirty work, yet today demonstrations of threshing by enthusiasts for the old ways not only attract crowds of onlookers but also former farmworkers happy to turn the clock back for a day. (SPS 11713)

Section Five

CATTLE AND SHEEP

Until the 1950s many Suffolk farms were mixed, with a cattle or dairy enterprise as well as an arable side. Here cattle are driven along the road by the cowman at Tattingstone; a tranquil rural scene which has all but disappeared from the county. (SPS 7624)

Men and boys going milking at Culpho, each carrying his own stool and 3 gallon pail, early twentieth century. This is one of a number of quarter-plate negatives depicting activities mainly on the Culpho Hall estate which were given to the SPS in 1957. Hand milking was still done on a good many farms as recently as the 1930s. (SPS 424)

The introduction of milking machines greatly eased the task of milking a herd of cows; these Red Polls at Laurel Farm, Felixstowe, are well used to having the cups placed on their teats. An American milking machine was shown at the 1862 International Exhibition, but it was not until the 1920s that all problems were overcome and machine milking became popular among farmers. (SPS 6202)

Some farmers with small dairy herds sold milk at the door. One such was L.W. Pudney, of Shrubbery Farm, Charsfield. When in the early thirties he began to deliver milk to customers it was one of his farmhands, George Mead, who became the roundsman, taking the milk in a churn on his bicycle (above left; SPS 7387). Later George graduated to a motor-cycle (above right; SPS 7388) and then to a small Ford van (below; SPS 7390). Deliveries came to an end in about 1940, when problems of petrol rationing, shortage of workers and wartime restrictions made them uneconomic.

In the towns milk rounds were introduced much earlier. William Hunt set up his dairy business in Felixstowe Road, Ipswich, in about 1910, later expanding into the bakery business as well. In his early days milk was measured out to customers from the churn or from a smaller can brought to the door. (SPS 1532)

Shearing sheep in a barn early this century. During the nineteenth century breeders in Suffolk were crossing the old Norfolk black-face sheep with other breeds to produce a type of animal deriving 'a large frame, hardihood, strength of constitution, and wonderful milking qualities from the old Norfolk blood, quality from the Southdown, and early maturity, good feeding characteristics, and heavy fleeces from the improved Lincoln or Cotswold' (*Livestock Journal*, July 1875). The Suffolk Sheep Society was formed in 1886. (SPS 17946)

Sheep dipping at Rattlesden, *c.* 1895. The use of various solutions such as lime and sulphur, carbolic acid and soft soap, and tobacco and sulphur, to guard against infestation with mites causing such afflictions as sheep scab, has a long history. (SPS 1880)

A lambing yard at Brent Eleigh made up from straw bales. Such temporary yards gave the ewes and their new-born lambs protection from the weather. An old handbook states that the site of hayricks and corn stacks was often determined with a view to affording a convenient supply of hay and straw to the flocks during the winter, and especially at lambing time, with as little carting as possible. (SPS)

A delightful picture of shepherd Albert Driver at Gosbeck Hall with two lambs, late 1940s or 1950s. The days when much of the coastal area of Suffolk was composed largely of sheep walks are long past, but sheep are still found on the county's farms, and the Suffolk breed is well represented at agricultural shows. (SPS 7843)

Section Six

SUGAR BEET

Although a sugar factory was built at Lavenham in 1868, little beet was grown in Suffolk until the new generation of factories came into existence in this century. These women are seen hoeing sugar beet at Great Blakenham in about 1914. Left to right: Miss Lafflin, Mrs Peter Belmont, whose husband worked at the Great Blakenham mill, Mrs Pilborough, Mrs Bumpstead, Mrs Gillingham. (SPS 7410)

Broadcasting fertilizer for the growing of sugar beet, which became an important crop in Suffolk after the building of the sugar factory at Ipswich in the 1920s. (SPS 8581)

Topping and carting sugar beet at Darmsden Hall, near Needham Market. Left to right: S. Francis, N. Chambers, B. Thorpe, -?-, F. Overton. (SPS 64430)

Lifting and topping sugar beet at Hoo Hall, 1933. The men are wearing sacking tied round the knees and in some cases makeshift aprons made of sacks, and one man, third from left, is seen knocking two beet together to knock off the earth. The growing of sugar beet was particularly labour-intensive. (SPS 7392)

Overleaf: Colinette Gallienne, of Brook Farm, Kettleburgh, a member of the Women's Land Army during the Second World War, hoeing beet. (SPS 13127)

Section Seven

BLACKSMITHS AND WHEELWRIGHTS

The forge was vital to the farming community in an age when everything depended on the horse; it was also very often a community meeting place. This photograph is of the smithy at Otley, with Dennis Stebbings on the right. The boy wears an old army uniform, even to the puttees; some wore their own uniform after discharge, but it seems likely this one had belonged to an elder brother. (SPS 11062)

Harry Burch outside the forge at Butley at the beginning of the century. At this period Edward Burch, perhaps his father, was listed as the blacksmith, but Harry took over the business in about 1914. There is evidence in the photograph of the operations of Jacob Cole, billposter, of Theatre Street, Woodbridge. (SPS 2311)

Frederick Crapnell, the Grundisburgh blacksmith, shoeing a horse in the 1920s. This horse seems well used to being shod, but a colt being shod for the first time could cause the smith a lot of trouble; hence it was customary in Suffolk for the farmer to pay for beer for the smith and his helpers when a horse was first shod. The Grundisburgh smithy closed in the 1970s, and was moved in its entirety to the Museum of East Anglian Life at Stowmarket, where it is often in use for demonstrations. (SPS 7766)

When war broke out in 1914 many farm horses were taken for the army. In this photograph of the forge at Great Livermere a number of army horses are being shod at Samuel Gathercole's forge. A good many horsemen were broken-hearted when animals to whom they were deeply attached were commandeered for war service. Not only were many horses killed in France, but in the army they were by no means as well looked after as on the farm. (SPS 7060)

The blacksmith did much more than look after the shoeing of horses, for he was in many cases something of an agricultural engineer as well. Joe Bugg, the Old Newton smith, is seen here operating a pillar drill. (SPS 2285)

Joe Bugg at Old Newton with a set of tractor-drawn crab harrows made for Philip Woodward. The blacksmith was always able to turn his hand to the repair of farm implements, and sometimes to the making of them. (SPS 2283)

Opposite: The same blacksmith at the forge, working the bellows with his left hand. (SPS 2284)

Robert Thain shoeing a horse at Bramfield. The Thains, Edward William and Robert, were adaptable men; they are listed in old directories from the beginning of the century as blacksmiths and cycle agents, while in the twenties they added 'agricultural implement manufacturers and agents' to the list of their accomplishments. (SPS 100)

Christopher Bedwell, the wheelwright at Earsham, 1907. Actually Earsham is on the Norfolk side of the Waveney, but as it is only just to the west of Bungay and very much part of the Waveney valley it seemed quite proper to include this fine photograph. Notice the size of the nave, or hub; this wheel has been made to fit a wooden axle. (SPS 743)

Vic Mortlock, of Lavenham, measuring a new wheel for the tyre using a 'traveller', *c.* 1958. Frank Mortlock & Sons were agricultural engineers of considerable local repute, as well able to replace the tubes of a traction engine boiler as to tyre a wheel. (SPS 1553)

The making of a wheel is a specialized operation, but one in which the blacksmith has his part to play. It is the smith who makes and fits the iron tyre that not only provides a hard-wearing periphery to the wheel but holds the wooden wheel together when in use. In October 1955 Brandeston blacksmith Hector Moore made and fitted tyres to wheels for Smyth seed drills, and Mrs Moore took a series of photographs showing the process. In this picture Hector Moore is examining one of the tyres; behind him are two 4 inch wheels and a 1½ inch wheel. (SPS 1517)

Bildeston forge: the tyre is being welded (above; SPS 1954) and carried out to be placed over the wheel on the tyring platform (below; SPS 1955). There are differences in detail between the way it is being done in these two photographs and the way it was done at Brandeston.

Hector Moore with a pair of gripes fits the heated tyre over the wheel (above; SPS 1515). To prevent the tyre dropping too low on one side three iron spikes have been driven into the felloes (pronounced fellies). The hot iron is burning the felloes, so Don Smith is ready with the watering can to cool it down. Hector and Tom Card use large hammers to set the tyre to the wheel (below; SPS 1514).

As Tom Card uses his hammer to ensure that the spokes are properly set in the nave and felloes Hector Moore screws down the nave to make sure the wheel does not 'go like an umbrella' (above; SPS 1516). Working on opposite sides of the wheel, Hector and Tom ensure the wheel is set up tight (below; SPS 2289).

Section Eight

WOODLAND TRADES

William Arbon's sawmills on The Green at Mendlesham, 1919. There were more than a score of timber merchants in the county at the beginning of this century, most of them small village concerns like the one shown here. The Arbons were carpenters and wheelwrights, but old William branched out into the timber trade at the beginning of the century. (SPS 6653)

Although Suffolk did not have large tracts of forest before the setting up of the Forestry Commission and the planting of great areas of conifers, the timber trade nevertheless played an important part in the economy of the county. To mention only one local industry, shipbuilding depended to a large extent on home-grown timber. In this photograph of about 1910 woodland workers are seen at Bramfield; it would appear that they are engaged in coppicing, the old practice of cutting underwood trees almost to ground level so that they grow again from the stools. (SPS 2310)

The sawpit at Mellis, near Eye, *c.* 1900. Before the coming of steam the traditional way of sawing a log into planks was on the sawpit, with the top sawyer on the log and the other sawyer below in the pit. (SPS 7841)

Overleaf: A portable engine driving a circular saw at an unidentified sawmills, possibly at Dallinghoo. The winch in front of the engine could be used to draw timber past the saw; if the operator tried to draw the timber too quickly the saw could snag and throw even a large piece of timber into the air with great force. In a few places windmills were used to power saws, usually circular saws, but no photographs of wind-powered sawmills seem to have survived, at least in Suffolk. Water power was also used, and one water sawmill has survived in Norfolk. (SPS 5361)

Barking a felled tree. The bark was peeled off to be sold to the tanners, using barking irons or peelers; the man on the right is using a body iron to strip the bark from the trunk, while others have wrong irons to take the bark from the branches, termed 'wrongs' in the trade. Note that this tree has been felled without the use of a crosscut saw; the butt shows clear evidence that only axes have been employed. (SPS 7853)

A timber jim with a large log suspended being hauled across Battery Green, Lowestoft, by a horse drawing a four-wheeled trolley, *c.* 1953.

Woodcutters splitting logs at Hintlesham, October 1949. It has been suggested that they might be splitting a walnut tree, the wood being used for rifle stocks. (SPS 2645)

A timber yard at Buxhall, seen in a detail from a photograph probably dating from the 1890s. Because of the long exposure necessary it has been posed with the 'action' frozen. Notice the absence of guards on the saws in this photograph; health and safety regulations were unknown in those days, and many a worker lost fingers or even a hand as a result of an accident. Many of the estates and some larger farmers had their own sawmills, and this is typical. (Sparkes)

The Sudbury timber yard of Wheeler & Westoby, who at the time of this photograph, late last century, were described as auctioneers and estate agents, timber, slate and cement merchants, sawmill proprietors, cabinet makers, upholsterers and undertakers. The firm still exists as Wheelers Ltd, though it has moved from King Street to a site at Chilton, on the outskirts of the town.

A hurdlemaker at Darsham, where members of the Snell family were hoop and hurdlemakers for the best part of a century. This is possibly James Rowe Snell, who was still operating in the forties. (SPS 5017)

Opposite: Russell Podd, the Otley hurdlemaker, at work in the 1970s. Hurdles were still in demand for making temporary sheep pens and for similar purposes. He would also turn his hand to other tasks such as thatching stacks (see p. 55).

A caterpillar tractor belonging to A.K. Cooper clearing timber at Glevering, near Wickham Market, 1937. Such tractors could do the work of several horses, yet there are still situations in which a horse has the advantage. (SPS 11039)

Section Nine

THE FISHERIES

An important part in the East Anglian fishery was played by the Scots 'girls', seen here at the farlanes. Before beginning work they would help each other to bind up their fingers with strips of linen, not to guard against the razor-sharp gipping knives but to enable them to hold the slippery herrings. Injuries from the knives were all too frequent, and the Church of Scotland operated a dressing station staffed by a nurse on the pickling plots to deal with such casualties. (SPS 7956)

There have been fishermen working off the Suffolk coast for at least 1,000 years, some of them making the long voyage to Icelandic and Faeroese waters and others working the inshore waters, never proceeding far from their home villages. In the Middle Ages it is difficult to separate fishermen from traders, for those who went to Iceland, like the men of Henry Tooley's ship *The Mary Walsingham*, which departed from Ipswich several times in the 1530s 'by the Grace of God Icelandwards', traded with the Icelanders for stockfish as well as catching their own.

In more recent times the herring fishery, which had been carried on at Lowestoft and elsewhere for hundreds of years, assumed a new importance as a result of the building of the railways, which opened up new inland markets. At Lowestoft and in certain nearby villages a way of life grew up that was firmly based on the herring industry with all its ramifications. There were nets to be made and to be repaired; fish to be smoked as well as cured in brine or packed in ice for export; fishing boats to be built in the local shipyards, sails to be made in the sail lofts, spars to be made; and hard ship's biscuits to be baked by the bakers.

There were fortunes to be made, too, even if those who made them were a tiny minority of the total employed in the fishing trade. When a trade grew up in iced herring for export to the Continent it proved so successful that it became known as klondyking; those merchants who took part became richer than most who went to the Klondyke in search of gold in 1897–8.

As steam took over in the fishing fleet the men of Lowestoft took to circumnavigating the British Isles in search of herring, going first to the West Country ports, then to Ireland or Milford Haven, to the Western Isles and the Shetlands, returning to East Anglia along the east coast in time for the Home Fishing in the autumn.

From Aldeburgh sailed the smacksmen who fished with lines for cod, which they brought back alive in the wet wells of their smacks. And from Lowestoft other smacksmen using trawl nets explored the North Sea in search of prime fish which went to Billingsgate and other markets by rail.

The herring fishery died out by 1960, and the trawl fishing industry has now been regulated almost out of existence. Only in old pictures and in old men's memories can the great days of Suffolk's fishing industry be recreated.

With the expansion of the industry Southwold sought to take advantage of growing congestion at Lowestoft by attracting drifters to its own harbour. A new quay was built and a herring saleroom erected, but the coming of war in 1914 brought an end to Southwold's hopes.

Large numbers of Scots 'girls' came in September by special trains from the west and east coasts of Scotland for the Home Fishing, which could be expected to peak at the November full moon. Their job was to gut the herring and pack them in barrels which were filled with brine; other Scots workers, men as well as women, would be employed in the smokehouses producing kippers, bloaters and even good red herring.

The herring fishing was a way of life in Lowestoft and in several of the neighbouring communities. The fishing industry benefited greatly from the building of the railways, which provided a means of reaching markets in the booming industrial towns of the Midlands. When this photograph was taken on the Lowestoft fish market at the beginning of this century the fishery was expanding towards its zenith in 1913. (SPS)

Opposite: This attractive youngster is carrying herring to the farlanes, where they were both gutted and sorted according to size at a great speed. It was very hard as well as skilled work, carried on almost entirely in the open at the time this photograph was taken in 1902.

By the end of the fishing in the 1950s many of the 'girls' were no longer young, for the new generation could see the decline gathering pace. While many were employed on the pickling plots there were also gutting houses in the town to which the herring were brought by lorry from the market.

Opposite: When a barrel was full it was filled with brine and stood on end. The fish would settle, and the head would then be removed so that the barrel could be topped up; it then had to be refilled with brine, as we see here. Barrels of pickled herrings, the so-called Scotch cure, were exported to northern Europe and to Russia by steamships which loaded in Lowestoft harbour.

The thousands of barrels needed to pack the herring were made by coopers, such as these working in Lowestoft, *c.* 1910. Some were local men, others Scotsmen who came down with the fishworkers by special train at the beginning of the season and returned home before Christmas, to be ready for the New Year. The man in the foreground is using a straight-paned hammer to chamfer a hoop to fit a tapering tub.

Stacking some of the many barrels needed during the Home Fishing to pack herrings for export. During the great days of the fishing, vessels brought cargoes of barrel staves from the Baltic for the Lowestoft coopers.

Making a drift net on a net loom at Sunrise Works, Lowestoft, late 1940s. Successful net looms were developed between 1820 and 1850 following the invention of the first such loom by James Patterson, of Musselburgh. With the decline of the herring fishery Sunrise Works closed down in the 1960s.

A great many women found employment as beatsters (from the Old English betan, to make good or repair) and netmakers in Lowestoft, Pakefield and Kessingland. These beatsters are seen in a Lowestoft netstore.

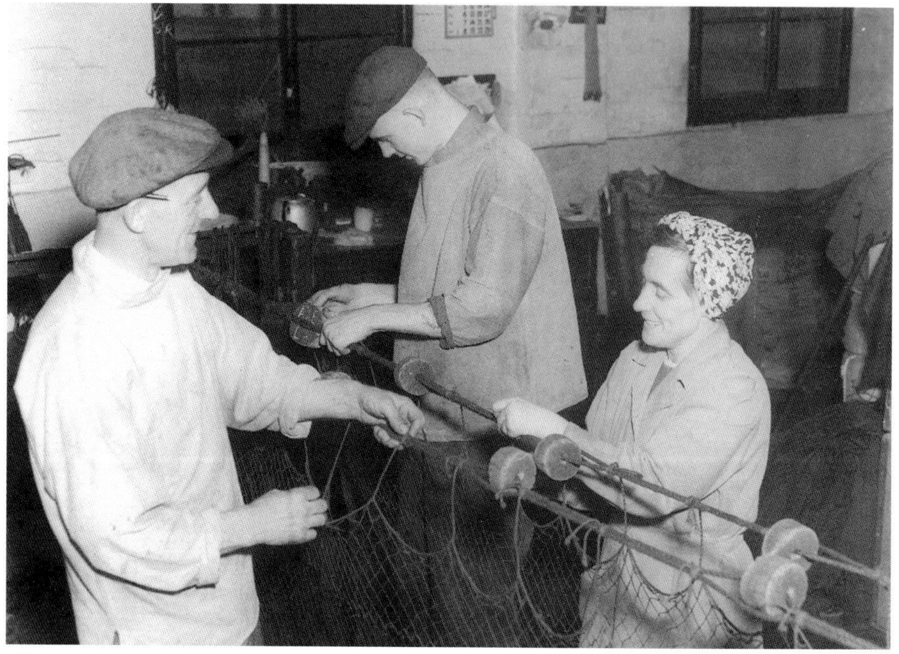

The men who set up the net, putting on the norsels and rigging the cork rope along the head of the net, were known as ransackers, from an old word of Norse origin meaning to search. Here a net is being set up after repair. The beatster is lending a hand.

As well as the crews of the fishing boats there was a whole army of shore workers not only preparing and packing the herring for onward transmission to home and export markets but also providing the many back-up services required by a fleet of hundreds of steam and sailing drifters. Here beatsters are repairing drift nets in the beating chamber.

At Lowestoft the netstores were mainly built of brick or flint, the largest of them being found along Whapload Road (the Warp Road Way in earlier times). The oldest of them, dating back to Tudor times, was burnt down some years ago. In Kessingland the netstores were different, being built of weatherboarding on timber frames.

The crew of the steam drifter *Sunny Bird* stowing the nets while in harbour. Just ahead of the wheelhouse can be seen a stack of buffs, the inflated canvas buoys which are attached to the net to keep it afloat.

Cleaning fish boxes on the market at Lowestoft on a quiet morning.

After repair the nets had to be tanned in the tan copper to preserve them, and they were then taken on to the Denes to be dried. A few of the rails on which they were hung still survive.

Another view of the *Sunny Bird*'s crew overhauling the nets. The man fourth from left is coiling the herring warp, the main rope by which the nets are hauled in.

A steam drifter makes its way to sea on a hazy Sunday morning in the 1950s. Lowestoft boats streamed out of harbour on a Sunday morning after the Saturday night layby, but Scots boats always remained in port for the Sabbath.

The Co-operative Wholesale Society had a canning factory in Waveney Drive, Lowestoft, in which herring were cooked and tinned. The factory had originally been built for Maconochie Brothers. (East Anglian Film Archive)

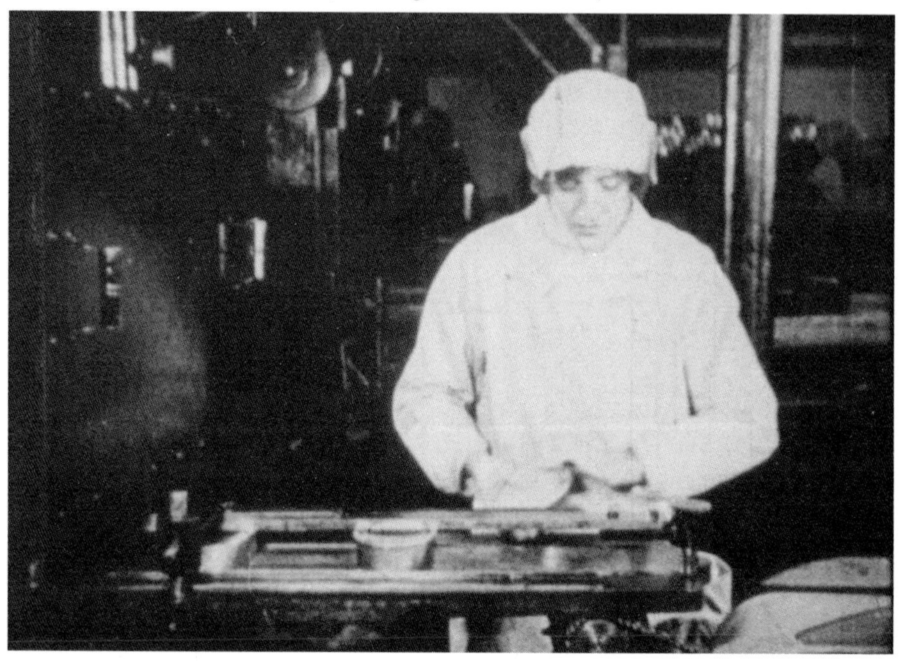

In earlier days the cans had been soldered up by hand, but by the time the CWS factory opened much of the work was done by machinery. (East Anglian Film Archive)

Labelling the sealed cans of herring, a job which was still done by hand. (East Anglian Film Archive)

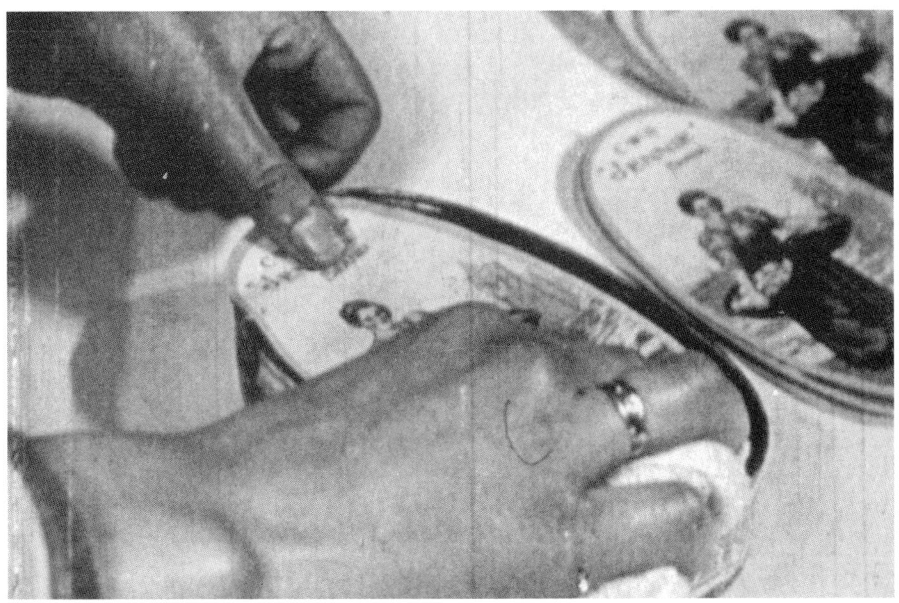

The label, bearing a picture of a Scots herring lassie. It is said that labels from Maconochie cans were used as currency in parts of Africa in the early part of the century. (East Anglian Film Archive)

A smack on her way out of harbour. The steam comes not from an auxiliary engine but from the steam capstan, used for warping the smack out of harbour as well as for hauling the trawl when at sea.

Sparmakers at work in a Lowestoft workshop in the 1950s. When the fishing fleet was made up entirely of sailing vessels, and most merchant ships were also working under sail, the sparmakers were busy men, not only making masts and yards and other spars for new ships but repairing the damage caused by bad weather and accidents. (SPS 2923)

A sparmaker using a drawknife to shape a mast. They also used a large axe, and when I took these photographs in a workshop on Battery Green, Lowestoft, I was told of an accident in which, to avoid the fingers of a child picking up woodchips for firelighting, a sparmaker turned the axe into his own leg. (SPS 2902)

Lowestoft became the most important fishing port in Suffolk after the construction of the harbour in the first half of the nineteenth century. Sailing drifters, or 'luggers' as they were called by the fishermen, are seen being towed out of harbour by the GER tug *Imperial*, *c.* 1900.

The Lowestoft trawling smacks of the late nineteenth and early twentieth century were fine ketch-rigged craft well able to keep the sea in almost any weather. They fished with a beam trawl, a net whose mouth was extended by a wooden beam with iron trawl heads at each end which held the beam above the sea bottom.

At sea on a steam trawler out of Lowestoft. The trawlers brought back fish such as cod, roker (skate), plaice, soles and dogfish, a species of small shark which the fishermen called simply 'dawgs'. (East Anglian Film Archive)

Steam trawlers began to take over from the smacks many years before the last of the smacks disappeared. Indeed, a number of new smacks were built in the 1920s both at Lowestoft and in the West Country to replace those lost during the First World War. Among the earliest steam trawlers in the Lowestoft fleet were old 'fleeters' from the Humber, some of them built of iron in the closing years of the nineteenth century. (East Anglian Film Archive)

Two motor trawlers lie in the Trawl Basin as the stern trawler *Universal Star*, the first stern trawler to join the Lowestoft fleet, turns to enter the Waveney Dock. At the time it seemed that the local fishing fleet was to be revolutionized; instead it has merely declined.

BRITAIN IN OLD PHOTOGRAPHS

To order any of these titles please telephone Littlehampton Book Services on 01903 721596

ALDERNEY

Alderney: A Second Selection, *B Bonnard*

BEDFORDSHIRE

Bedfordshire at Work, *N Lutt*

BERKSHIRE

Maidenhead, *M Hayles & D Hedges*
Around Maidenhead, *M Hayles & B Hedges*
Reading, *P Southerton*
Reading: A Second Selection, *P Southerton*
Sandhurst and Crowthorne, *K Dancy*
Around Slough, *J Hunter & K Hunter*
Around Thatcham, *P Allen*
Around Windsor, *B Hedges*

BUCKINGHAMSHIRE

Buckingham and District, *R Cook*
High Wycombe, *R Goodearl*
Around Stony Stratford, *A Lambert*

CHESHIRE

Cheshire Railways, *M Hitches*
Chester, *S Nichols*

CLWYD

Clwyd Railways, *M Hitches*

CLYDESDALE

Clydesdale, *Lesmahagow Parish Historical Association*

CORNWALL

Cornish Coast, *T Bowden*
Falmouth, *P Gilson*
Lower Fal, *P Gilson*
Around Padstow, *M McCarthy*
Around Penzance, *J Holmes*
Penzance and Newlyn, *J Holmes*
Around Truro, *A Lyne*
Upper Fal, *P Gilson*

CUMBERLAND

Cockermouth and District, *J Bernard Bradbury*
Keswick and the Central Lakes, *J Marsh*
Around Penrith, *F Boyd*
Around Whitehaven, *H Fancy*

DERBYSHIRE

Derby, *D Buxton*
Around Matlock, *D Barton*

DEVON

Colyton and Seaton, *T Gosling*
Dawlish and Teignmouth, *G Gosling*
Devon Aerodromes, *K Saunders*
Exeter, *P Thomas*
Exmouth and Budleigh Salterton, *T Gosling*
From Haldon to Mid-Dartmoor, *T Hall*
Honiton and the Otter Valley, *J Yallop*
Around Kingsbridge, *K Tanner*
Around Seaton and Sidmouth, *T Gosling*
Seaton, Axminster and Lyme Regis, *T Gosling*

DORSET

Around Blandford Forum, *B Cox*
Bournemouth, *M Colman*
Bridport and the Bride Valley, *J Burrell & S Humphries*
Dorchester, *T Gosling*
Around Gillingham, *P Crocker*

DURHAM

Darlington, *G Flynn*
Darlington: A Second Selection, *G Flynn*
Durham People, *M Richardson*
Houghton-le-Spring and Hetton-le-Hole, *K Richardson*
Houghton-le-Spring and Hetton-le-Hole: A Second Selection, *K Richardson*
Sunderland, *S Miller & B Bell*
Teesdale, *D Coggins*
Teesdale: A Second Selection, *P Raine*
Weardale, *J Crosby*
Weardale: A Second Selection, *J Crosby*

DYFED

Aberystwyth and North Ceredigion, *Dyfed Cultural Services Dept*
Haverfordwest, *Dyfed Cultural Services Dept*
Upper Tywi Valley, *Dyfed Cultural Services Dept*

ESSEX

Around Grays, *B Evans*

GLOUCESTERSHIRE

Along the Avon from Stratford to Tewkesbury, *J Jeremiah*
Cheltenham: A Second Selection, *R Whiting*
Cheltenham at War, *P Gill*
Cirencester, *J Welsford*
Around Cirencester, *E Cuss & P Griffiths*
Forest, The, *D Mullin*
Gloucester, *J Voyce*
Around Gloucester, *A Sutton*
Gloucester: From the Walwin Collection, *J Voyce*
North Cotswolds, *D Viner*
Severn Vale, *A Sutton*
Stonehouse to Painswick, *A Sutton*
Stroud and the Five Valleys, *S Gardiner & L Padin*
Stroud and the Five Valleys: A Second Selection, *S Gardiner & L Padin*
Stroud's Golden Valley, *S Gardiner & L Padin*
Stroudwater and Thames & Severn Canals, *E Cuss & S Gardiner*
Stroudwater and Thames & Severn Canals: A Second Selection, *E Cuss & S Gardiner*
Tewkesbury and the Vale of Gloucester, *C Hilton*
Thornbury to Berkeley, *J Hudson*
Uley, Dursley and Cam, *A Sutton*
Wotton-under-Edge to Chipping Sodbury, *A Sutton*

GWYNEDD

Anglesey, *M Hitches*
Gwynedd Railways, *M Hitches*
Around Llandudno, *M Hitches*
Vale of Conwy, *M Hitches*

HAMPSHIRE

Gosport, *J Sadden*
Portsmouth, *P Rogers & D Francis*

HEREFORDSHIRE

Herefordshire, *A Sandford*

HERTFORDSHIRE

Barnet, *I Norrie*
Hitchin, *A Fleck*
St Albans, *S Mullins*
Stevenage, *M Appleton*

ISLE OF MAN

The Tourist Trophy, *B Snelling*

ISLE OF WIGHT

Newport, *D Parr*
Around Ryde, *D Parr*

JERSEY

Jersey: A Third Selection, *R Lemprière*

KENT

Bexley, *M Scott*
Broadstairs and St Peter's, *J Whyman*
Bromley, Keston and Hayes, *M Scott*
Canterbury: A Second Selection, *D Butler*
Chatham and Gillingham, *P MacDougall*
Chatham Dockyard, *P MacDougall*
Deal, *J Broady*
Early Broadstairs and St Peter's, *B Wootton*
East Kent at War, *D Collyer*
Eltham, *J Kennett*
Folkestone: A Second Selection, *A Taylor & E Rooney*
Goudhurst to Tenterden, *A Guilmant*
Gravesend, *R Hiscock*
Around Gravesham, *R Hiscock & D Grierson*
Herne Bay, *J Hawkins*
Lympne Airport, *D Collyer*
Maidstone, *I Hales*
Margate, *R Clements*
RAF Hawkinge, *R Humphreys*
RAF Manston, *RAF Manston History Club*
RAF Manston: A Second Selection, *RAF Manston History Club*
Ramsgate and Thanet Life, *D Perkins*
Romney Marsh, *E Carpenter*
Sandwich, *C Wanostrocht*
Around Tonbridge, *C Bell*
Tunbridge Wells, *M Rowlands & I Beavis*
Tunbridge Wells: A Second Selection, *M Rowlands & I Beavis*
Around Whitstable, *C Court*
Wingham, Adisham and Littlebourne, *M Crane*

LANCASHIRE

Around Barrow-in-Furness, *J Garbutt & J Marsh*
Blackpool, *C Rothwell*
Bury, *J Hudson*
Chorley and District, *J Smith*
Fleetwood, *C Rothwell*
Heywood, *J Hudson*
Around Kirkham, *C Rothwell*
Lancashire North of the Sands, *J Garbutt & J Marsh*
Around Lancaster, *S Ashworth*
Lytham St Anne's, *C Rothwell*
North Fylde, *C Rothwell*
Radcliffe, *J Hudson*
Rossendale, *B Moore & N Dunnachie*

LEICESTERSHIRE

Around Ashby-de-la-Zouch, *K Hillier*
Charnwood Forest, *I Keil, W Humphrey & D Wix*
Leicester, *D Burton*
Leicester: A Second Selection, *D Burton*
Melton Mowbray, *T Hickman*
Around Melton Mowbray, *T Hickman*
River Soar, *D Wix, P Shacklock & I Keil*
Rutland, *T Clough*
Vale of Belvoir, *T Hickman*
Around the Welland Valley, *S Mastoris*

LINCOLNSHIRE

Grimsby, *J Tierney*
Around Grimsby, *J Tierney*
Grimsby Docks, *J Tierney*
Lincoln, *D Cuppleditch*

Scunthorpe, *D Taylor*
Skegness, *W Kime*
Around Skegness, *W Kime*

LONDON

Balham and Tooting, *P Loobey*
Crystal Palace, Penge & Anerley, *M Scott*
Greenwich and Woolwich, *K Clark*
Hackney: A Second Selection, *D Mander*
Lewisham and Deptford, *J Coulter*
Lewisham and Deptford: A Second Selection, *J Coulter*
Streatham, *P Loobey*
Around Whetstone and North Finchley, *J Heathfield*
Woolwich, *B Evans*

MONMOUTHSHIRE

Chepstow and the River Wye, *A Rainsbury*
Monmouth and the River Wye, *Monmouth Museum*

NORFOLK

Great Yarmouth, *M Teun*
Norwich, *M Colman*
Wymondham and Attleborough, *P Yaxley*

NORTHAMPTONSHIRE

Around Stony Stratford, *A Lambert*

NOTTINGHAMSHIRE

Arnold and Bestwood, *M Spick*
Arnold and Bestwood: A Second Selection, *M Spick*
Changing Face of Nottingham, *G Oldfield*
Mansfield, *Old Mansfield Society*
Around Newark, *T Warner*
Nottingham: 1944–1974, *D Whitworth*
Sherwood Forest, *D Ottewell*
Victorian Nottingham, *M Payne*

OXFORDSHIRE

Around Abingdon, *P Horn*
Banburyshire, *M Barnett & S Gosling*
Burford, *A Jewell*
Around Didcot and the Hagbournes, *B Lingham*
Garsington, *M Gunther*
Around Henley-on-Thames, *S Ellis*
Oxford: The University, *J Rhodes*
Thame to Watlington, *N Hood*
Around Wallingford, *D Beasley*
Witney, *T Worley*
Around Witney, *C Mitchell*
Witney District, *T Worley*
Around Woodstock, *J Bond*

POWYS

Brecon, *Brecknock Museum*
Welshpool, *E Bredsdorff*

SHROPSHIRE

Shrewsbury, *D Trumper*
Whitchurch to Market Drayton, *M Morris*

SOMERSET

Bath, *J Hudson*
Bridgwater and the River Parrett, *R Fitzhugh*
Bristol, *D Moorcroft & N Campbell-Sharp*
Changing Face of Keynsham,
B Lowe & M Whitehead
Chard and Ilminster, *G Gosling & F Huddy*
Crewkerne and the Ham Stone Villages,
G Gosling & F Huddy
Around Keynsham and Saltford, *B Lowe & T Brown*
Midsomer Norton and Radstock, *C Howell*
Somerton, Ilchester and Langport, *G Gosling & F Huddy*
Taunton, *N Chipchase*
Around Taunton, *N Chipchase*
Wells, *C Howell*
Weston-Super-Mare, *S Poole*
Around Weston-Super-Mare, *S Poole*
West Somerset Villages, *K Houghton & L Thomas*

STAFFORDSHIRE

Aldridge, *J Farrow*
Bilston, *E Rees*
Black Country Transport: Aviation, *A Brew*
Around Burton upon Trent, *G Sowerby & R Farman*
Bushbury, *A Chatwin, M Mills & E Rees*
Around Cannock, *M Mills & S Belcher*
Around Leek, *R Poole*
Lichfield, *H Clayton & K Simmons*
Around Pattingham and Wombourne, *M Griffiths, P Leigh & M Mills*
Around Rugeley, *T Randall & J Anslow*
Smethwick, *J Maddison*
Stafford, *J Anslow & T Randall*
Around Stafford, *J Anslow & T Randall*
Stoke-on-Trent, *I Lawley*
Around Tamworth, *R Sulima*
Around Tettenhall and Codsall, *M Mills*
Tipton, Wednesbury and Darlaston, *R Pearson*
Walsall, *D Gilbert & M Lewis*
Wednesbury, *I Bott*
West Bromwich, *R Pearson*

SUFFOLK

Ipswich: A Second Selection, *D Kindred*
Around Ipswich, *D Kindred*
Around Mildenhall, *C Dring*
Southwold to Aldeburgh, *H Phelps*
Around Woodbridge, *H Phelps*

SURREY

Cheam and Belmont, *P Berry*
Croydon, *S Bligh*
Dorking and District, *K Harding*
Around Dorking, *A Jackson*
Around Epsom, *P Berry*
Farnham: A Second Selection, *J Parratt*
Around Haslemere and Hindhead, *T Winter & G Collyer*
Richmond, *Richmond Local History Society*
Sutton, *P Berry*

SUSSEX

Arundel and the Arun Valley, *J Godfrey*
Bishopstone and Seaford, *P Pople & P Berry*
Brighton and Hove, *J Middleton*
Brighton and Hove: A Second Selection, *J Middleton*
Around Crawley, *M Goldsmith*
Hastings, *P Haines*
Hastings: A Second Selection, *P Haines*
Around Haywards Heath, *J Middleton*
Around Heathfield, *A Gillet & B Russell*
Around Heathfield: A Second Selection,
A Gillet & B Russell
High Weald, *B Harwood*
High Weald: A Second Selection, *B Harwood*
Horsham and District, *T Wales*
Lewes, *J Middleton*
RAF Tangmere, *A Saunders*
Around Rye, *A Dickinson*
Around Worthing, *S White*

WARWICKSHIRE

Along the Avon from Stratford to Tewkesbury, *J Jeremiah*
Bedworth, *J Burton*
Coventry, *D McGrory*
Around Coventry, *D McGrory*
Nuneaton, *S Clews & S Vaughan*
Around Royal Leamington Spa, *J Cameron*
Around Royal Leamington Spa: A Second Selection,
J Cameron
Around Warwick, *R Booth*

WESTMORLAND

Eden Valley, *J Marsh*
Kendal, *M & P Duff*
South Westmorland Villages, *J Marsh*
Westmorland Lakes, *J Marsh*

WILTSHIRE

Around Amesbury, *P Daniels*
Chippenham and Lacock, *A Wilson & M Wilson*
Around Corsham and Box, *A Wilson & M Wilson*
Around Devizes, *D Buxton*
Around Highworth, *G Tanner*
Around Highworth and Faringdon, *G Tanner*
Around Malmesbury, *A Wilson*
Marlborough: A Second Selection, *P Colman*
Around Melksham,
Melksham and District Historical Association
Nadder Valley, *R. Sawyer*
Salisbury, *P Saunders*
Salisbury: A Second Selection, *P Daniels*
Salisbury: A Third Selection, *P Daniels*
Around Salisbury, *P Daniels*
Swindon: A Third Selection, *The Swindon Society*
Swindon: A Fourth Selection, *The Swindon Society*
Trowbridge, *M Marshman*
Around Wilton, *P Daniels*
Around Wootton Bassett, Cricklade and Purton, *T Sharp*

WORCESTERSHIRE

Evesham to Bredon, *F Archer*
Around Malvern, *K Smith*
Around Pershore, *M Dowty*
Redditch and the Needle District, *R Saunders*
Redditch: A Second Selection, *R Saunders*
Around Tenbury Wells, *D Green*
Worcester, *M Dowty*
Around Worcester, *R Jones*
Worcester in a Day, *M Dowty*
Worcestershire at Work, *R Jones*

YORKSHIRE

Huddersfield: A Second Selection, *H Wheeler*
Huddersfield: A Third Selection, *H Wheeler*
Leeds Road and Rail, *R Vickers*
Pontefract, *R van Riel*
Scarborough, *D Coggins*
Scarborough's War Years, *R Percy*
Skipton and the Dales, *Friends of the Craven Museum*
Around Skipton-in-Craven, *Friends of the Craven Museum*
Yorkshire Wolds, *I & M Sumner*